Owned by God

Paul's Pastoral Strategy
in 1 Corinthians

Michael B Thompson

Associate Principal, Ridley Hall, Cambridge
and Lecturer in New Testament
for the Cambridge Theological Federation

GROVE BOOKS LIMITED
RIDLEY HALL RD CAMBRIDGE CB3 9HU

Contents

Acknowledgments

I wish to thank Philip Jenson for his helpful comments on a rough draft of this booklet; I alone am responsible for the views expressed here. This booklet is dedicated to R C 'Dick' Henderson and Harold W Hoehner, two great shepherds already in glory.

First Impression June 2017
ISSN 1365–490X
ISBN 978 1 78827 012 0

Introduction

Imagine that you are a pastor of a congregation of less than a hundred adults; perhaps that is not so difficult to do! Beginning with a small core, you have laboured in a pioneer ministry for a year and a half, building up a fledgling church in a cosmopolitan centre. But while you are away, seconded to ministry in another place, you hear distressing news. Your original church is having serious problems and they need your help.

They are dividing into factions over different Christian personalities. Some members are super-spiritual and arrogant. A few even go so far as to advocate ending marital relations; others are known to be using prostitutes, and one apparently influential member is committing incest with his stepmother. At least one of your people is publicly humiliating another in court. Some are emphasizing their personal freedom to the detriment of others. Worship services for your congregation are a mess; people are drawing attention to themselves by what they wear or do not wear and by how much they speak in tongues. Instead of sharing food when they gather, one person gets drunk while another goes hungry. Some of them are saying that it does not matter what they do with their bodies because there will not be a resurrection anyway.

Now if you were their pastor and circumstances dictated that you could only *write* to such a congregation, how would you start your letter? Where would you begin and what would be your strategy in responding? What would you say about your readers to help to move them forward?

If you were their pastor, how would you start your letter?

The apostle Paul faced that very dilemma in Ephesus, as he looked west across the Aegean Sea and pondered how to help his young congregation in Corinth. This booklet looks closely at the initial verses in 1 Corinthians to see what they can teach us about how Paul the pastor began to respond to a group of Christians with multiple, serious problems. What we discover may well surprise us and challenge some of our instincts, as we seek direction and wisdom to be faithful followers of Christ.

2 Kinship Language

The salutations (initial greetings) in Paul's letters share several common elements and the temptation in Bible study to speed over them is great. But the small differences in salutations give us clues about particular themes Paul goes on to address later in the letter and how he will address his people's problems. They reveal his mood and what is on his mind. Although his self-identification in 1 Cor 1.1 is unremarkable when compared with his other letters, his addition of Sosthenes as a co-sender and the description of him as our 'brother' signal at the very beginning that Paul wants to remind the congregation at Corinth that they were part of a wider family.

In Acts 18 we read of a Sosthenes who was a leader in the synagogue at Corinth. When Gallio dismissed the case brought by Jews in the city against Paul, the crowd beat this man (18.17). Perhaps he was sympathetic to Paul's preaching and eventually became a Christian; 1 Cor 1.1 is the only other reference to a Sosthenes in Scripture. What is clear is that Paul expects the Corinthians to know the man he refers to as a *brother* in Christ.

Kinship language features frequently in 1 Corinthians

Kinship language features frequently in 1 Corinthians. Paul uses 'brother' (*adelphos*) 39 times in the letter, almost a third of all of the instances in the Pauline corpus (133 times)! He likes to call his readers 'brothers,' and of course in the absence of evidence to the contrary we should normally understand the inclusion of women as 'sisters' when he speaks this way, as more modern translations indicate.[1]

Paul uses this kinship language at the beginning of sections in the letter when he is introducing a new thought (so on divisions 1.10f; on his preaching 2.1; on divine discipline 10.1; on spiritual gifts 12.1; on resurrection 15.1). He also does it when concluding a subject (on remaining in the state in which they were called 7.24; on the Lord's supper 11.33; on worship 14.39). He does it when making a point in correction (not many being wise or noble 1.26; inability to speak to them as spiritual people 3.1; not being puffed up 4.6; not being children in their thinking 14.26). He does it when distinguishing his hearers from non-Christians (regarding marriage 7.12, 14f) or urging them to consider right attitudes towards each other (discipline 5.11). He reminds them of their sibling relationship in the case of taking another Christian to court and even wronging them in the first place (6.5f, 8).

Paul uses 'brother' repeatedly in 1 Corinthians 8 to emphasize how *unthinkable* it should be to exercise personal liberty at the expense of another for whom Christ died (8.11f, 13 *twice*). Calling his hearers 'brothers' strengthened the bond of friendship and affection as well as kinship (15.31). It added great weight when he wanted to say something very important (15.50; 16.15). It was apparently Paul's favourite, default way of referring to other Christians (15.12; 16.20).

That little word 'brother' is something we should not pass over quickly

That little word 'brother,' therefore, is something we should not pass over quickly. Jesus himself taught his disciples to think of themselves in family terms not based on bloodline but on shared obedience to God (Mark 3.31–35; Matt 12.46–50). It is true that language of fictive kinship (social ties that were not established by blood or marital relationship) was common among ethnic and religious groups in the first century, but Paul's starting point here is a reminder not of sentiment but of a reality—an established relationship that does not depend on feelings. Belonging to each other as Christians derives from a fundamental belonging to God our Father.

Many Christians today deliberately continue to use the language of 'brother' (and 'sister'); others ignore it, as do modern translations in some passages (*eg* the NRSV translation of Matt 18.15; 25.40; Luke 6.41f). Perhaps in the sophisticated West we have come to find such language as embarrassing or claiming a relationship that we do not feel or live up to. When we ignore this way of speaking, we lose sight of something that has the potential in the long term of drawing us together and deepening connections between us. It is given to us as an important part of our identity in Christ. Paul did not wait for feelings to dictate whether he should address others in kinship language given by God. Sometimes it takes time for emotions to catch up with truth.

Mary Birge has studied 1 Corinthians 3–6 and chapter 14 in particular, focusing on kinship 'across class, economic, and social boundaries' as a key to Paul's rhetorical strategy.[2] She sees kinship language appearing in other forms besides sibling imagery. Paul also uses the language of parent and child to describe his relationship with his hearers (3.1f; 4.14–16), and he speaks of members of a household including the steward (*oikonomos*), the servant (*diakonos, hypēretēs*) and co-workers/builders (*sunergoi*) in 3.5–9; 4.1; ch 14. In all of this he appeals to kinship for teamwork for building up rather than tearing down. In effect, if not in purpose, he is rebuilding the Corinthians' sense of identity as those who belong together. It needed rebuilding, because their problems reflected a return to their old, pre-Christian values and identities as isolated individuals shaped by their city and its culture.

A strong sense of belonging to a healthy family is often missing in our modern world. Alienation, divorce, abuse, increased mobility and the lure of technology are only a few of the factors that can contribute to pull people apart. The more we immerse ourselves in advertising-driven media of various kinds, the more we encounter a world view that that reinforces a fundamental identity for us as separate consumers making independent choices. As a result, it becomes increasingly easy for us to make those choices without awareness of how they affect other people. This 'atomisation' in society fosters selfishness and also makes it harder for us to discover the joy of serving others and of deepening life-giving relationships.

Instead of seeing ourselves as belonging to a positive network of permanent, giving relationships, we are being formed by our culture as isolated individuals seeking to get the most out of what we can. Adopting a biblical model of kinship language may seem quaint, but for Paul and other early Christians it was acknowledging something foundational in building up a living, thriving fellowship of faith. How we address each other in Christ may seem a small thing. It may feel strange, odd or even untrue. But it has a bonding effect on relationships, just as does calling someone we meet by their own name.

Questions for Thought

- Can you think of other passages in the New Testament that reflect the practice of calling fellow Christians a brother or sister?

- What differences could it make if you really believed that the people sitting around you in church were your brothers and sisters?

- What does the imagery of belonging to a family say about how we should relate to other professing Christians with whom we radically disagree?

- Is there a positive step you could take in your church to help foster your congregation having a sense of being family?

Owned by God

At least four more striking features emerge from a close reading of Paul's description of the Corinthian congregation in v 2.

Paul's first description of his hearers in 1 Corinthians is 'the church *of God.*' He only adds 'of God' (*tou theou*) to 'church' nine times in all of his letters, but five of the occurrences are here in 1 Corinthians (1.2; 10.32; 11.16, 22 and 15.9). The only time he uses the phrase in a salutation is to the Corinthian congregation (here and in 2 Cor 1.1). They are *God's* church, although they are not acting like it. They *belong* to God, and Paul will go on to develop that theme repeatedly in different ways in the letter.[3]

A Greek notion of wisdom (cleverness) was a prize in Corinth

The possessive genitive 'of God' speaks directly to the danger that the Corinthians were in from forming factions to which they claimed to belong: 'I am *of* Paul,' 'I am *of* Apollos,' and 'I am *of* Cephas' (1.12; *cf* 3.4). They appear to have been concerned about who baptized them and were seeking to improve their status by identifying with the one they considered the *wisest* and most impressive leader (1.13–17).

A Greek notion of wisdom (cleverness) was a prize in Corinth because the city lay only a few miles down the road from Athens, the great cultural centre of Greece and home of a long line of influential philosophers. As a major crossroads for trade, Corinth was a bustling place of commerce and travellers passing through; the city had a reputation for vice, but lacked a long tradition that it could be proud of. With its florid style, Corinthian architecture attempted to compensate for this inferiority complex, and the city was full of structures built to bring praise and glory to their builders. But to be seen as *wise* was an ultimate value—to have honour in a relatively shallow local culture.

Some Corinthians no doubt identified with Cephas (Peter) because he travelled with Jesus who taught him directly and gave him special status and authority. Others were impressed with Apollos' rhetorical skill and powerful speech (see Acts 18.24–28). Still others lifted up Paul, perhaps emphasizing that he had founded the Corinthian church, giving them an initial dose of Christian wisdom. The cult of the personality is nothing new!

Paul's corrective response underlines that *God's* wisdom seen in the cross is wiser and stronger than any mere human leadership can offer (1.18–25). The people the Corinthians are making so much of are only servants working for and with God to build something far greater than themselves. God is the one who gives the growth (3.7) and with a threefold possessive genitive *theou* ('of God,' in the emphatic position in the Greek text) Paul makes it clear that God is their owner; he is the one to whom his human co-labourers belong, and the church is God's field and God's building (3.9). That specific building is the living temple—the very shrine of God (3.16f). Paul goes on to turn their notions of belonging to mere humans upside down in the following verses. At the climax of this stage in his argument, he tells them that instead of them belonging to particular leaders, all things belong to the Corinthians (3.21f), and they belong to Christ, and Christ to God (3.23). The unity that is in danger of being undermined by a focus on particular leaders/personalities can be strengthened by everyone remembering their shared allegiance to the one in whom they will inherit everything.

This theme of belonging continues in various forms through the letter

This theme of belonging in the sense of ownership continues in various forms through the letter (as we shall see), but most notably reappears in 6.19. There, in the context of discussion of the right use of their bodies, Paul explicitly adds, 'you are not your own,' citing the reason 'for you were bought with a price' (6.20). Addressing the temptation to try to change one's condition to gain status he repeats the words again in 7.23: 'you were bought with a price,' reminding both slaves and free that they belong ultimately to Christ the Lord in whose service they find greatest freedom (7.22). Repetition is an important clue as to what really matters to a writer; by repeating 'bought with a price' Paul is emphasizing that his readers are owned by the Lord who purchased them by his very death.

Undergirding this imagery of purchase is the rich theme of redemption from bondage in Egypt, so that the people of Israel would belong to and serve the God of Abraham (*cf* Isa 43.1). Yet even before that redemption, God owned all things. Arguably Paul's starting point is the belief inherited from his Jewish heritage that 'The earth is the Lord's and the fullness thereof' (Ps 24.1), a verse that he quotes in 1 Cor 10.26. It is another text in which a possessive genitive (*tou kuriou*) stands in the emphatic position. From the very start of creation, *to God* everything belongs.

Near the end of his letter, in his discussion of the resurrection Paul returns to this language of belonging. 'For as all die in Adam, so all will be made alive in Christ,' he writes, 'But each in his own order: Christ the first fruits, then at his coming those who belong to Christ' (15.22f). Here again we find the possessive genitive used to describe those who are 'of Christ' (*hoi tou Christou*). Although our awareness and experience of being owned by God varies in this life, Paul sees the fullness of that ownership worked out in our resurrection. All of this began with Paul's addressing his readers as the church *of* God. His strategy for correcting their waywardness is essentially one of reminding them not simply who, but more profoundly *whose,* they are.

Individually and corporately, Christians need a frequent reminder that we are not autonomous, independent or isolated. We are people who are not our own. We belong to someone else; someone far more powerful, trustworthy and capable of guiding and delivering us from whatever lack we may face.

Questions for Thought

- With what different images does the Bible teach that God has a claim on your life?

- What might be some of the implications of belonging to God?

- If we do not belong to God, to whom do we belong?

- What difference could a strong sense of belonging to God make for your congregation?

4

Set Apart for God

Returning to the salutation in 1 Corinthians we find another distinct and programmatic claim that reveals Paul's strategy of building Christian identity. But given the circumstances of the church in Corinth, this one is perhaps the most surprising and contrary to what most Christians think: *the Corinthians are already holy*. Notice that Paul does not say that they are not acting holy or must be holy or will be holy, but that they *are* holy. They have already been sanctified, made holy in Christ Jesus. He is not addressing a subset of the congregation, a select group of pious and obedient people. He is talking to all of them. In all of the letters from Paul that we possess this is the only time he uses the verb 'to sanctify' in a salutation, and the perfect tense here points to a completed action with an ongoing result. To emphasize this truth, he repeats the Greek root, adding that they are 'called to be *saints*.'[4]

One of Paul's favourite description for Christians was 'saints'

One of Paul's favourite description for Christians was 'saints,' 'holy ones' (see 1 Cor 6.1f; 14.33; 16.1, 15 and every undisputed Pauline letter except Galatians).[5] They are set apart for God as his own and so belong to him. But only in 1 Corinthians do we get a *double* affirmation of the holiness of the readers in the salutation ('sanctified,' 'saints'), and yet their behaviour reflected anything but holiness! Rather than with imperatives to *be* holy or to *act* holy, Paul begins with the indicative, the indisputable *fact* of their holiness.[6] Their status as holy began when they became Christians.

The translation 'called *to be* saints' is misleading if we read it as indicating something only potential or future, although I suspect many readers instinctively take it that way. As more literal translations will indicate, the words 'to be' are not in the Greek text. He is not implying that they are not yet holy, just as he would not want the Corinthians to think that because he was 'called *to be* an apostle' he was not yet an apostle (1.1)! He certainly was one. In the phrase he is affirming two definite things: they are called (discussed in the next chapter of this booklet) and they are holy.

People often think of holiness as essentially a very strict purity typical of only a few; for some it can even have negative connotations. In the history of the church the desire to be completely set apart has led people to an isolated lifestyle. The pursuit of holiness for some Pharisees meant keeping away from people and things that could lead to defilement and impurity. Being set apart can be taken negatively as essentially being set apart *from* the world. Yet Jesus was able to socialize with outcasts and those viewed as far from holy without endangering or losing his own holiness. He knew that he belonged to God and was set apart *unto* his Father to do his Father's will. Precisely because he was dedicated to God and secure in the knowledge of *whose* he was, he was free to act in faith rather than to recoil in fear.

The roots of this language are again found in the Old Testament. Holiness of course has its starting point in the character of God. God is holy (Isa 6.3), other, different, set apart, not like us (Ps 50.21), special, unique. In Deut 7.6 we read why the Israelites were told not to have anything to do with other gods:

> For you are a people holy to the Lord your God; the Lord your God has chosen you out of all the peoples on earth to be his people, his treasured possession.

Israel had become a holy people at Sinai, despite being as imperfect, confused and disobedient as the Corinthians (Exod 19.5f). The truth that God had already set apart his people to be holy, his own special channel of blessing to the rest of his creation, was part of the foundation for giving them particular direction. His people are holy in that sense whether or not they consider themselves to be so.

Most Christians are too humble to think of themselves as holy. We see holiness in terms of 'ought' or 'should'—a lofty status that only few can attain. I regularly puzzle my students by prefacing their name with the word 'Saint'; it sounds so foreign to them to hear themselves called 'Saint Nigel' or 'Saint Fiona.' Although they will go on to preach sermons on All Saints' Day reminding their people that all Christians are saints, learning to consider themselves on a daily basis as already holy is not intuitive. Perhaps the reluctance is rooted in a sense of failure, or of fear that considering oneself to be holy will lead

Our growth in holiness develops out of being a holy people

to arrogance or an air of superiority; certainly that was not Paul's intention. Our growth in holiness develops out of the givenness of being a holy people. In the Old Testament, God chose a people to be his holy possession, and that identity brought with it security, direction and an incentive to live as a holy people. Precisely because they were *already* holy and owned by God, Paul could go on to appeal to his congregation to act in a positive way as a holy people with a special purpose.

Holiness is a theme that features again significantly at critical points in 1 Corinthians. In Corinthian culture, one way of increasing personal status was through boasting; the Corinthians were boasting in Cephas, Apollos and Paul. Repeating the same root for holiness, Paul goes on to remind his hearers that God is 'the source of your life in Christ Jesus, who became for us wisdom from God, and righteousness and *sanctification* and redemption,' so that any boasting should be in the Lord, not in human wisdom or leaders (1.30). For Christians, being sanctified has its roots in what Christ, God's holy one, has accomplished for us (John 6.69).

Paul returns to the theme of holiness again in 3.17 at the climax of discussion about God's building project, the church: 'God's temple is *holy* and you are that temple.' Because the living temple is holy and belongs to God, it should be absolutely unthinkable to act in ways that would tear it down or destroy its unity.

The Greek verb reappears in 6.11 when Paul reminds the Corinthians in the hinge between his discussion of lawsuits and immorality that they were washed, they were *sanctified*, they were justified in the name of the Lord Jesus Christ and in the Spirit of God.[7] They cannot act in the way they used to act because in an important sense they are no longer the people they used to be. Being holy closes down some old options, but also opens up new possibilities, as reflected in the life of Christ. The saints, Paul says, will judge the world (6.1f). The children of a Christian are holy; they belong to one who in turn belongs to God (7.14).

The sanctification or holiness of which Paul repeatedly speaks here is not a possibility but a reality to which he appeals. They have been set apart as belonging to God; they are his, and getting that fact back into their thinking is part of Paul's pastoral strategy for reforming their sense of Christian identity.

Questions for Thought

- When have you ever thought of yourself as holy?

- What do you think is the biblical connection between holiness and purity?

- What differences could a strong collective notion of being holy make for your congregation?

- Must such a belief inevitably lead to a sense of superiority or arrogance?

Called by God

5

A third feature of the salutation, already noted, is the readers' *calling*.[8] They are 'called to be saints' (1.2). 'Calling' language is not unusual in Paul, but it is more common in 1 Corinthians than in any other letter (the verb *kaleō*, the adjective *klētos* and the noun *klēsis* together appear 17 times!). Concluding his initial thanksgiving, Paul reminds his hearers in 1.9 that they were called by God into the fellowship of his Son, Jesus Christ. That reflects Paul's tendency to use 'calling' language with reference to people becoming Christians.

Our modern tendency is to understand calling in individualistic terms and referring to particular roles in employment, but for Paul, calling signals a transfer into a new community and a new identity. In his fine study, *Conversion at Corinth*, Stephen Chester observes, 'Paul conceives calling as granting a new identity as part of the people of God. In doing so he again draws upon the Septuagint, where God calls his people back to him, and back to their true identity.'[9]

Correcting the Corinthians' focus on human wisdom in ch 1, Paul states, '… Jews demand signs and Greeks desire wisdom, but we proclaim Christ crucified, a stumbling block to Jews and foolishness to Gentiles, but to those who are *the called*, both Jews and Greeks, Christ the power of God and the wisdom of God' (1.22–24). The 'called' here are identical to those who believe but the language of calling highlights God's saving initiative in contrast to human wisdom (1.21). Before the Corinthians chose to follow particular human leaders, the choice that really mattered was God's gracious calling of them.

Paul develops this further in the following verses when he states,

> Consider your own call, brothers and sisters: not many of you were wise by human standards, not many were powerful, not many were of noble birth. But God chose what is foolish in the world to shame the wise; God chose what is weak in the world to shame the strong; God chose what is low and despised in the world, things that are not, to reduce to nothing things that are, so that no one might boast in the presence of God.' (1.26f)

Calling and choosing language here are closely related. Although Christians continue to differ over the relationship of divine sovereignty and human

"

choice, Paul would not want us to miss that he is correcting Corinthian arrogance. He is making the larger point that his readers belong fundamentally to God rather than to the world and its values (*cf* Lev 20.24; Deut 9.5–6). The effect is to foster humility and a sense of identity and belonging that in turn will give direction to the choices they make in life.

Calling language appears ten times in ch 7, where Paul addresses matters about which some in the church had written to him (7.1). Perhaps influenced by the teachings that in the resurrection there is no marrying or giving in marriage (Mark 12.25) or that some had made themselves eunuchs for the sake of the kingdom (Matt 19.12), apparently some of his people thought that they should live a more ascetic lifestyle and end sexual relations in their marriage or even separate from their spouse. Where his hearers were inclined to think that changes in their circumstances were the way to increase their status and put them in a better spiritual position, Paul urges faithful living in their existing marital relationships. In a case where an unbelieving partner wanted to separate, God's calling of the believing partner still meant a call to be peaceable (*cf* Rom 12.18), regardless of how we understand the notion that the believer is not 'bound' (1 Cor 7.15).

In 7.17–24 Paul highlights that God's calling to belong to his people was more important than changes people might seek to effect in their circumstances. He writes,

> …let each of you lead the life that the Lord has assigned, to which God *called* you. This is my rule in all the churches. Was anyone at the time of his *call* already circumcised? Let him not seek to remove the marks of circumcision. Was anyone at the time of his *call* uncircumcised? Let him not seek circumcision…Let each of you remain in the *condition* (*klēsei, calling*) in which you were *called*.
>
> Were you a slave when *called*? Do not be concerned about it. Even if you can gain your freedom, make use of your present condition now more than ever. For whoever was *called* in the Lord as a slave is a freed person belonging to the Lord, just as whoever was free when *called* is a slave of Christ. You were bought with a price; do not become slaves of human masters. In whatever condition you were *called*, brothers and sisters, there remain with God.

Here Paul begins by stating the principle (7.17), before illustrating it with respect to circumcision (7.18–19). He then restates the principle (7.20), illustrates it once more with slavery (7.21–23) and finally repeats the principle yet again (7.24). Paul's repetition of calling language is striking. However we are to understand his advice about a slave gaining freedom in 7.21, clearly Paul wants his hearers to think of themselves as people on whose lives God has the first and primary claim. They are not to revert to their former bondage to an honour-shame culture where status is determined only in human eyes and based on human choices.[10] They have been called, and they belong to God.

I suspect that one reason we hear little teaching about calling (and choosing) language in the Bible is the scandal of particularity and the problem of theodicy. It immediately raises the questions 'Why us?' and 'Why not them?' These are natural questions, but the biblical themes of calling and election were not given to explain fully God's purposes (if we could understand them we would *be* God), to satisfy curiosity and certainly not to justify exclusion of others. Instead, such language should lead us to humble gratitude for what we have received and to commitment to share what we have received with others. Calling and election is to become a channel of blessing to the wider world.

It is worth pondering to what extent our Christian congregations are being reminded week by week of having been individually and collectively *called* by God. A sense of call can remind us that God is a person who loves us, wants us to know him, and takes initiatives with us. He has a plan and can be trusted; it is not simply a matter of our independent choices. His call brings with it direction, new possibilities and options for life, as well as closing down avenues and choices that lead to frustration and futility.

Questions for Thought

- How did God call you to be a Christian?

- What does it mean to 'consider your calling' (1 Cor 1.26)? What effect should that have on you?

- Should we avoid calling/choosing language today because of the difficulties it creates for those outside the church?

6 Together with All of the Churches

A fourth programmatic feature in v 2 of the salutation is less tied to specific vocabulary but is summed up in the words 'together with all' (*sun pasin*) who call upon the name of the Lord. A recurring thought that appears in various forms in the letter is that the hearers are not alone as individuals or as a church, but are a part of a larger communion of churches that belong to Christ. This is reiterated by the words 'in every place' in v 2, to make it clear that the Corinthian church, in the words of Anthony Thiselton, is *'not a self-sufficient community; they are not the only pebble on the beach.'*[11]

On top of this Paul awkwardly adds the Greek words 'theirs and ours' at the end of v 2. Although these adjectives could refer to 'their place and our place,' it is more likely that they refer to 'their Lord and ours,' the point being that the Corinthians share a common belonging to the same Lord. The threefold emphasis of 'together with all,' 'in every place' and 'theirs and ours' is unique to the salutation of 1 Corinthians.[12] A church obsessed with autonomy, personal choice and individualistic liberty needed to hear from the outset that they were part of something larger and accountable to the same Lord.

> **A church obsessed with autonomy needed to hear from the outset that they were accountable**

And so it is not surprising that at various places in the letter Paul draws their attention to the practice in the wider communion to which they belong. In 4.17, as he begins to conclude his discussion of the major issue of divisions in the church, he speaks of Timothy, who has come to remind them of Paul's ways in Christ Jesus, 'just as I teach them everywhere (*pantachou*) in every (*pasē*) church.' We have already seen that after stating his principle that each should live their life as the Lord has assigned it and as God has called in 7.17, he adds, 'This is my rule in all (*pasais*) the churches.' In 11.16 he concludes his discussion of the exegetically vexed issue of head covering with the words, 'But if anyone is disposed to be contentious—we have no such custom, nor do the *churches* of God.' In 14.33 Paul appeals again to the practice 'as in all (*pasais*) the churches of the saints' as an incentive for the Corinthians to return to good order in their worship; he repeats the plural 'churches' in the following verse.[13] Outside of 1 Corinthians the phrase 'all the churches' appears only in 2 Cor 8.18; 11.28 and Rom 16.4, 16.

A real danger for the Corinthian Christians was to see their choices, individually and collectively, as free from obligation or responsibility towards each other. Paul's references to all of the churches and his language of 'ways,' 'rule' and 'custom' reminded them that with God's gifts there came identity as belonging to a larger body of Christians, all offering a common allegiance to Christ as Lord.

I have often thought it curious how many churches in the country of my birth (the US) have in their names the word 'Independent.' By that they are emphasizing that they are not part of any larger denomination, membership in which they see as a disadvantage. Indeed, the notion of 'independence' is a cultural fundamental in America because of our history. But the danger of Christian 'independence' is an unhelpful isolation and a profound susceptibility to error (as well as a poor witness to the wider love of Christ). There are problems and errors in every denomination, but independent churches are particularly susceptible to corruption through the power and false teaching of individuals. Membership in the larger alliance of Christ's people can bring a vital and needed sense of accountability, as well as security and solidarity. If anything, Paul would have wanted the Corinthians to be known as a 'Dependent' church—dependent upon Christ and the rest of his people to whom they belonged.

Thus far we have highlighted five features (four of them unique) in the salutation of 1 Corinthians, and all of them are positive. Because they have become Christians, the Corinthians are members of a family; they belong to God as part of *his* church. They have been set apart as his holy people, belonging to him. They have been called by God to belong to him. And they are part of a larger association that includes all of the churches in every place who acknowledge Christ to be their Lord. Three more striking features in the letter's opening verses deserve brief attention before we attempt to draw our observations together and offer a conclusion.

Questions for Thought

- Does your church claim to belong to a larger visible association of Christians? What difference does that make in the life of the congregation?

- Are there ways that you or members of your church can play a greater role in the life of that larger community of churches?

- If your church considers itself to be an 'independent' church, what can be done to help to foster closer relationships with other groups of Christians in your area?

7 Three More Vital Pastoral Themes

In the Lord Jesus Christ

It is remarkable how often at the outset of this letter Paul refers explicitly to Christ (Jesus) or Jesus Christ—four times in the first three verses and a total of ten times in the first ten verses. Six of these include the words 'our Lord.' Paul did not practice mindless repetition. His language reflects no poverty of ideas but a concern to turn a wayward congregation's eyes away from themselves and their issues to the one in whom their true unity, hope and direction was founded. Every time Paul went on to use the expression 'our Lord' (1.10; 5.4 twice; 9.1; 15.31, 57) or 'our God' (6.11) he was reinforcing for his hearers that they all belonged together in a common allegiance.

'In Christ Jesus' (*en Christōi Iēsou*; 1.2, 4) is a distinctive feature of Paul's theology. In its various forms it is arguably *the* characteristic expression of belonging (1.30; 3.1; 4.10, 15, 17; 15.18f). For James Dunn, 'Paul's perception of his whole life as a Christian, its source, its identity, and its responsibilities, could be summed up in these phrases.'[14] J Bryan Tucker has observed in his recent study, *You Belong to Christ*, that Paul wants the Corinthians to see it as the foundation for their social identity.[15] With its wide range of nuances the phrase is too large a topic to explore here; the Greek preposition *en* can signify many things but often it connotes 'in the sphere of,' *ie* belonging to the one who has brought deliverance.[16] In any case, it is, in fact, the final phrase in Paul's letter and reflects the identity given to his readers (16.24).

God's Gracious Faithfulness

It is striking that a letter to a congregation with so many presenting problems even has a thanksgiving after the salutation. Normally Paul finds something to thank God for before he launches into the body of the epistle. He did not feel he always had to; in Galatians he was so hopping mad that he dispensed with it and jumped into the issues with both feet. But in 1 Corinthians there is a thanksgiving and it is rather fulsome. Look at it more closely, however, and you will see that Paul is not flattering his congregation with false praise. In fact there is nothing that the Corinthians have done or are doing that he gives thanks for here, unlike his commendation of the Thessalonians' work of faith, labour of love and steadfastness of hope (1 Thess 1.3).

Instead, Paul is recounting what God has done and will do that has made the difference for them. God has given grace, enriching them in speech and knowledge (1.5), confirming Paul's gospel among them (1.6) and providing no lack of gifts as they wait for Christ to be publicly revealed (1.7). God will keep them strong to the end so that they will be blameless on that day (an astonishing statement in view of their issues addressed in the letter! [1.8]). In short, the God who called them to belong to him is the faithful one (1.9)—another truth reiterated later in the letter to help them when they are tempted (10.13). He is working to give them growth and bring them to their goal (*cf* 3.6; 4.7). He is the source of their life (1.30), his power their foundation (2.5), his wisdom their salvation (2.6–16) and his the victory (15.57).

Remarkably, Paul is confident about the future of the Corinthian Christians because he knows that God, not he, is ultimately their leader and sustainer. At the outset of this letter, Paul is making it very clear where their trust, confidence and allegiance must remain, yet without exhorting them to do so. He is establishing the facts (the indicative: God is faithful) before urging any action (the imperative: so be faithful to him and to each other).

Participation

Paul's thanksgiving concludes with the statement that through God's faithfulness they have been called into *fellowship* (*koinōnia*) with his Son Jesus Christ. Here we encounter yet another image of sharing and belonging. Although many today use the word to mean little more than social interaction, Paul had much more in mind. Anthony Thiselton translates *koinōnia* as 'communal participation.'[17] From other texts we see that for Paul, fellowship meant giving as well as receiving, active and sometimes costly involvement rather than simply sharing social pleasantries.

> **For Paul, fellowship meant active and sometimes costly involvement**

Although the apostle speaks of his readers' sharing in the gospel early in Philippians (1.5) and sharing their faith in Philemon 6, only in 1 Corinthians do we find him making the point at the outset of a letter that they have been called into fellowship. Paul will go on to emphasize the significance of *sharing* in the body and blood of Christ in 10.16; *cf* 10.18, 20. Because there is one bread that is shared, he writes, 'We who are many are one body, for we all partake of the one bread' (10.17). We find the theme of belonging again most clearly when Paul addresses the issue of spiritual gifts already alluded to in his thanksgiving (1.5). All of the Corinthians are members of one body (12.12f), and the analogy of different parts belonging to a physical body illustrates the importance of God-given diversity in the body of Christ in which Paul's hearers participate and belong (12.27).[18]

Paul does not seem to envision a church as a group of people in which the people up front do all of the sharing and the rest simply listen. *Everyone* is already given gifts that have the potential to help build up, in some way or other, the sharing community.

Questions for Thought

- Do you think of yourself and your congregation as being *in Christ*?

- How has the faithfulness of God in your life been manifested in the last year?

- Are there any in your church that are not aware of the gifts they have been given to bless others? What can be done to turn them loose to do so?

Paul's Pastoral Strategy

Morna Hooker has drawn attention to the way that Paul as pastor tended to draw his readers back to the relevance of the gospel itself through credal summaries such as those we find in Rom 1.3–4; 4.25; 1 Thess 4.14; Gal 2.20 and Philippians 2.[19] She has shown that Paul had a way of adapting traditional language about what God has done in Christ in order to address the particular needs of the addressees. A relatively new commentary on 1 Corinthians (by Ciampa and Rosner) emphasizes the role of the Old Testament in shaping Paul's pastoral response.[20]

At the outset of his letter, Paul is sounding out themes he will develop later on

Without denying the importance of those observations, here I have sought to show that at the outset of his letter, Paul is sounding out themes that he will pick up and develop in significant ways later on, as he seeks to help his people. Like any of us, he must have been disappointed, hurt and frustrated at the disintegration and confusion in his congregation. Having poured eighteen months and more of his own blood, sweat and tears into their lives, he must have been tempted to get right to the point and tell them directly all of the things they should or should not be doing.

Some of the first sermons that I hear from the students I teach who are preparing for ordained ministry follow that approach. They are heavily laden with sentences featuring the words 'must,' 'ought to,' 'should,' or, their favourite, 'need to.' The natural, human tendency is to moralize, to pile on helpful suggestions that we genuinely think will help people in our congregations become better Christians. Sometimes we say, 'I want to encourage you,' when what we mean is, 'I want to exhort you. I want to tell you what you need to do.' In doing so, of course, we are often simply preaching to ourselves, riding hobby horses, responding to crises without reflecting on an overall strategy in ministry and communication.

What I love about Paul is that he did not fit this mould. Yes, he will get on to specific issues, and he was perfectly able to speak in imperatives when he needed to, sometimes bluntly. But we have seen that he introduces his first letter to the Corinthians and undergirds his pastoral admonition with a positive emphasis that declares who his readers are and, most importantly, *whose* they are. They belong to someone and to something far greater and far more wonderful than they have imagined. They need reminding of a wonderful truth, clothed in various images: they belong to God and are owned as such by him to be his church.

Paul is engaged in forming, broadening, deepening and building up a new sense of identity. The Corinthians cannot live the way they used to live because they are not the people they used to be. They are under new ownership, new management, and they belong to a new community and a master whose values turned those of the cosmopolitan culture of Corinth on its head. They have not completely lost their old identity, and Paul does not expect them to change their personalities or their histories. But they are in the process of transformation, and their hope is rooted not in their own abilities but in what has been given by the grace of God in the person of their Lord Jesus Christ.

> **Paul is engaged in forming a new sense of identity**

Ten times in the letter Paul will ask the rhetorical question, 'Do you not know…?' Some of these refer to common knowledge that illustrates an important point (5.6; 6.16; 9.13, 24); others directly relate theological truths he had sought to teach his people during his ministry (*eg* 6.9). Five of the latter directly concern the hearers' identity. As they are in danger of sliding back into patterns of thought and behaviour from their inherited culture, Paul reminds them that they are God's temple and that his Spirit dwells in them (3.16), the saints will judge the world and angels (6.2f), their bodies are members of Christ, and their bodies are a temple of the Holy Spirit (6.15). They are not their own, but have been bought with a price (6.19). 'Do you not know?' he asks. His aim was to ensure that they did.

A Broad Overview of Paul's Pastoral Argument in 1 Corinthians

Having identified a number of key elements that characterize what Paul cites as givens in the salutation and thanksgiving prayer, we can now trace the overall shape of his response to the many problems in the church in Corinth. Notice how often the initial themes in 1.1–9 reappear as Paul goes about seeking to pastor his people in the rest of the letter.

In chapter 1, he urges unity and consideration of their calling, reminding them into whom they were baptized, that God's wisdom seen in the cross is greater than any human wisdom they could desire, and that God is the source of their life and the only person worthy of their boasting.

In chapter 2, he reminds them that their spiritual birth did not come through great oratory but through the power of the Spirit, that God's wisdom is

Spirit-enabled, and that they have been given the mind of Christ (by virtue of having that Spirit).

In chapter 3, he tells them that their quarrelling reflects spiritual infancy and that the men they are making much of are only servants. God is the source of real growth, and people are accountable to God for the effects of their actions on his building project, the holy temple that is the church. Boasting in leaders is foolish because all things belong to the Christians (as joint heirs with Christ) and they ultimately belong to God.

In chapter 4, he again reminds them that the messengers are only stewards and boasting is inappropriate since everything is ultimately a gift from God. He contrasts the arrogant attitude of the Corinthians with the apostolic sufferings in which he shares, and he appeals as a spiritual father to them to imitate him. He warns that he is aware of arrogant attitudes and will come soon.

In chapter 5, Paul questions them as to what their attitude should have been to the situation of incest and declares his judgment. He corrects the boasting by likening their circumstances to the cleaning out of yeast for Passover, appealing to the death of Christ. He clarifies that his earlier letter was not about associating with non-Christians but about the need for discipline among the believing community. They need to act accordingly!

In chapter 6, he challenges their real knowledge in taking one another to public court, reminding them of their destiny as judges of angels. Wrongdoers will not inherit the kingdom of God; in contrast, the Corinthians were washed in baptism, sanctified, justified in Christ and in the Spirit. Reminding them of their destiny as those to be raised and of the significance of sex as unitive, he argues against using prostitutes. He reminds them that fornication is sin against their own body and that their body is a temple belonging to God; they have been bought with a price and are his.

Paul desires a life free from anxieties and split allegiances

In chapter 7, Paul responds to their written questions by agreeing that celibacy is a beautiful thing but goes on to argue practically for wives and husbands to pay their full dues in relationship; abstinence should be only be temporary and under agreed conditions. Paul prefers singleness for the single and widowed, but the married should not separate from their partner—even if married to an unbeliever. They should thrive within the circumstances in which they were called, whether slave or free, or engaged. He desires a life free from anxieties and split allegiances. Marriage is good, even in the current, pressing eschatological circumstances, although Paul would prefer a simpler life for them.

In chapter 8, he urges that love builds up the community whereas knowledge puffs up, so, regarding food offered to idols, although there is only one God and Lord, the weak—for whom Christ died—are still in danger if the strong exercise their liberty to eat food that is tempting to the weak. The strong would then be sinning against their own brothers and sisters and so against Christ. Better to abstain!

In chapter 9 he offers his example. He reminds them that he is a *bona fide* apostle and so for many reasons has every right to be supported for his labours. But he refrains so as not to put an obstacle in the way of faith; he does not make full use of his rights. He becomes the slave of all to win all. Like a self-denying athlete pursuing the prize, he disciplines himself and does not cave in to bodily cravings.

In chapter 10 he draws on the OT example of the failure of God's people in the wilderness, reminding the Corinthians that spiritual privileges and blessings are no guarantee against failure. In their testing God is faithful and will provide a way out. So they should not participate in idol feasts (that is sharing with demons as the Lord's supper is a sharing in Christ). Although they are free they should seek advantage of the other and act wisely in various circumstances.

Everything should be to the glory of God so that people may be saved

Everything should be to the glory of God, not causing stumbling but so that people may be saved; they should imitate Paul as he imitates Christ.

In chapter 11 he corrects a disruptive issue of appearance in worship regarding head covering, basing this in Christ's relationship with God and appealing to the custom of all the churches. Then he corrects abuses at the Lord's supper, appealing to the fact that the church belongs to God. He reminds them of the significance of the words of institution as proclaiming the Lord's death; they should judge themselves in their behaviour towards each other and not overeat.

In chapter 12, he teaches that the same Spirit distributes the various gifts to each as he wills. They were all united into one in baptism and received the same Spirit. Each part is indispensable (especially the parts viewed as weaker), so that all care for each other, suffer together and rejoice together. God has appointed the various and different giftings.

In chapter 13 he teaches what should guide the exercise of these spiritual gifts: love for the other. Gifts without love are nothing; love, on the other hand, is positive, builds up (and is contrary to an arrogant attitude) and is greater even than faith or hope.

In chapter 14, he urges the pursuit of love in the communal exercise of gifts; the goal is the upbuilding of the body (God's temple). Uninterpreted tongues are unintelligible and do not build up other people. The presence of an interpreter is crucial for upbuilding; if they were a *sign* of anything, uninterpreted tongues were a sign to unbelievers! Order and peace should characterize the exercise of gifts by all for everyone's benefit. Disruptive questions from (untaught) wives should be answered at home and all should be done decently and in order.

In chapter 15 he corrects unbelief in the resurrection by taking them back to the heart of the gospel he preached, which included the resurrection of Christ himself. The logical consequence of Christ not being resurrected is that they are still in their sins. But Christ has been raised as we will be when he returns. Otherwise, why bother with suffering for Christ? Although questions remain about the nature of the body, the new body will be changed, spiritually renewed and immortal, meaning victory over sin and death. So knowing that future, they should remain steadfast in their faith.

In chapter 16, Paul reminds them to keep up with the collection for the saints in Jerusalem. He will come; Timothy may do so; Apollos will come when he can. They should stand firm, courageous, strong and all should be done in love. He gives various greetings, warns against not loving the Lord, prays for his coming and affirms his love for all of them in Christ.

Conclusion

In summary, Paul's *strategy* in 1 Corinthians as a pastor was to remind and teach his people about what God in Christ and through the Spirit had done in the past for them, was doing for them in the present, and would do for them in the future. God had already given them a status and identity as his own holy people. He was building the fellowship of his temple, the church. And ultimately he was going to defeat death by the gift of their transformed, resurrected bodies. The Corinthian Christians were owned by God, bought with the price of Christ's blood, and their new identity as a family and fellowship meant an end to old ways of estimating honour, worth and social status. Paul drew upon a wide range of available imagery to communicate the significance of God's many gifts to them. A challenge for us today is to learn from Paul's example and so be helped to enable God's people to grow in grace.[21]

Works Consulted

Mary Katherine Birge SSJ, *The Language of Belonging: A Rhetorical Analysis of Kinship Language in First Corinthians* (Leuven: Peeters, 2002).

Stephen Chester, *Conversion at Corinth: Perspectives on Conversion in Paul's Theology and the Corinthian Church* (London: T and T Clark, 2003).

Roy E Ciampa and Brian S Rosner, *The First Letter to the Corinthians* (Grand Rapids, MI: Eerdmans; Nottingham: Apollos, 2010).

J D G Dunn, *The Theology of Paul the Apostle* (Grand Rapids, MI: Eerdmans, 1998).

Victor Paul Furnish, 'Belonging to Christ: A Paradigm for Ethics in First Corinthians,' *Interpretation* 44/2, April 1990, 145–157.

Holmberg, Bengt (ed), *Exploring Christian Identity* (Tübingen: Mohr Siebeck, 2008).

Morna D Hooker, 'Paul the Pastor: The Relevance of the Gospel,' *Proceedings of the Irish Biblical Association* 31, 2008, 17–31.

David G Horrell, *Solidarity and Difference: A Contemporary Reading of Paul's Ethics* (London: T and T Clark, 2005).

Kar Yong Lim, 'Paul's Use of Temple Imagery in the Corinthian Correspondence: The Creation of Christian Identity' in Kathy Ehrensperger and J Brian Tucker (eds), *Reading Paul in Context: Explorations in Identity Formation: Essays in Honour of William S Campbell* (New York: T and T Clark, 2010) pp 189–206.

Anthony C Thiselton, *The First Epistle to the Corinthians: A Commentary on the Greek Text* (Grand Rapids, MI: Eerdmans; Carlisle: Paternoster, 2000).

J Bryan Tucker, *You Belong To Christ: Paul and the Formation of Social Identity in 1 Corinthians 1–4* (Eugene, OR: Pickwick, 2010).

Jan G Van der Watt (ed), assisted by François S Malan, *Identity, Ethics, and Ethos in the New Testament* (Berlin: Walter de Gruyter, 2006).

Notes

1 The Greek word for sister (*adelphē*) occurs only six times in the Pauline corpus (Rom 16.1, 15; 1 Cor 7.15; 9.5; 1 Tim 5.2; Philemon 2), always either with reference to specific women or in places where the word 'brother' would be inappropriate. 2 Cor 6.18 reveals a broadening of the male-focused (but nonetheless female-inclusive) language Paul inherited from 1 Sam 7.14 and his culture.

2 Mary Katherine Birge SSJ, *The Language of Belonging: A Rhetorical Analysis of Kinship Language in First Corinthians* (Leuven: Peeters, 2002) p. 2.

3 As we will go on to explore, Ciampa and Rosner see it emphasized in the threefold affirmations, 'The church of God in Corinth, to those sanctified, to those called to be holy' (Roy E Ciampa and Brian S Rosner, *The First Letter to the Corinthians* (Grand Rapids, MI: Eerdmans; Nottingham: Apollos, 2010)) p 6.

4 The English verb 'sanctify' and noun 'saint' translate the same Greek root rendered by the adjective 'holy.'

5 In addition to the cited texts from 1 Cor, see Rom 1.7; 8.27; 12.13; 15.25, 31; 16.2, 15; 2 Cor 1.1; 8.4; 9.1, 12; 13.12; Phil 1.1; 4.21f; 1Thess 3.13; Philemon 5, 7. See also Eph 1.1, 15, 18; 2.19; 3.5, 8,18; 4.12; 5.3; 6.18; Col 1.2, 4, 12, 22, 26; 3.12; 2 Thess 1.10; 1 Tim 5.10.

6 The only exception to this usage in 1 Corinthians is 7.34 with its reference to the concern of the unmarried woman and virgin to be holy in body and spirit.

7 However we are to understand the difficult statement that 'the unbelieving husband is made holy through his wife, and the unbelieving wife is made holy through her husband' in 7.14, the REB renders *hēgisastai* here 'belongs to God.'

8 For extended discussion, see Stephen Chester, *Conversion at Corinth: Perspectives on Conversion in Paul's Theology and the Corinthian Church* (London: T and T Clark, 2003) pp 59-112.

9 *ibid*, p 107.

10 Anthony C Thiselton, *The First Epistle to the Corinthians: A Commentary on the Greek Text* (Grand Rapids, MI: Eerdmans; Carlisle: Paternoster, 2000) p 562.

11 *ibid,* p 74; italics his.

12 The greeting in 2 Cor 1.1 adds 'including all the saints throughout Achaia.'

13 Because the words in 1 Cor 14.34–35 appear after v 40 in some manuscripts, some scholars think they did not originally come from Paul. No manuscript, however, omits the words entirely.

14 J D G Dunn, *The Theology of Paul the Apostle* (Grand Rapids, MI: Eerdmans, 1998) p 399.

15 J Bryan Tucker, *You Belong To Christ: Paul and the Formation of Social Identity in 1 Corinthians 1–4* (Eugene, OR: Pickwick, 2010) p 151.

16 For an overview, see Dunn, *op cit*, pp 396–401.

17 Thiselton, *op cit*, pp 103–105.

18 Other belonging imagery may be found in 'Our paschal lamb, Christ, has been sacrificed' (5.7) and 'Our ancestors were all under the cloud, and all passed through the sea...' (10.1–4).

19 'Pastor.'

20 Thiselton, *op cit*.

21 To be sure, not every letter from the apostle follows the pattern of 1 Corinthians; Paul's tactics varied in different circumstances, and some of his logic was very difficult to follow! But underlying and forming the basis for his exhortations and corrections remained the prior gifts of God to his people.